I Am Not

Written by Tanya Luther

Pop it in the bin.

Stop! I am not junk!

I can be lots of stuff.

Snip and stick!
I can be a puppet.

Dig and fill!
I can be a plant pot.

Bend me!
I can be a box.

Cut and tuck!
I can be a hat.

Criss-cross!
I can be a mat.

Add a tag!
I can be a gift bag.

Rip, rip!
I can be a soft bed.